Little Pebble™

Habitats

All About the North and South Poles

by Christina Mia Gardeski

raintree
a Capstone company — publishers for children

Raintree is an imprint of Capstone Global Library Limited, a company incorporated in England and Wales having its registered office at 264 Banbury Road, Oxford, OX2 7DY – Registered company number: 6695582

www.raintree.co.uk
myorders@raintree.co.uk

Edited by Nick Healy
Designed by Juliette Peters
Picture research by Wanda Winch
Production by Steve Walker
Originated by Capstone Global Library Limited
Printed and bound in China

ISBN 978-1-4747-4722-6
21 20 19 18 17
10 9 8 7 6 5 4 3 2 1

British Library Cataloguing-in-Publication Data
A full catalogue record for this book is available from the British Library

Acknowledgements
We would like to thank the following for permission to reproduce photographs: Dreamstime: Filigrin, 15, Twildlife, 11; Shutterstock: elxeneize, 21, FloridaStock, 5, Incredible Arctic, 19, La Nau de Fotografia, 9, MZPHOTO.CZ, 17, Photodynamic, cover, Sergey Uryadnikov, 1, Vladimir Melnik, 7, Volodymyr Goinyk, 13, zolssa, snowflake design.

Every effort has been made to contact copyright holders of material reproduced in this book. Any omissions will be rectified in subsequent printings if notice is given to the publisher.

Contents

Two poles. 4

The North Pole. 6

The South Pole. 12

Days and nights. 18

Glossary 22
Read more 23
Websites. 23
Index 24

Two poles

The Earth has two poles.

One pole is in the north.

The other is in the south.

The North Pole

The North Pole is in the Arctic.

It is a cold habitat.

Ice caps the ocean.

7

Polar bears live here.

Fur keeps them warm.

The snow is deep.

Foxes dig for food.

arctic foxes

11

The South Pole

The South Pole is in Antarctica.

It is cold here too.

Ice tops the land.

12

Penguins live here.

Feathers keep them warm.

A seal naps.

His belly is full of fish.

Days and nights

Winter is long at the poles.

The days are dark.

Summer is short.

The nights are sunny.

Life is cool at the poles!

Glossary

Antarctic   South Pole and the ring of land and ocean around it

Arctic   North Pole and the ring of land and ocean around it

habitat   home of a plant or animal

North Pole   northernmost end of the Earth

penguin   seabird with wings that can swim but cannot fly

polar bear   big, white bear that lives in the Arctic

pole   ring of land and ocean at the ends of the Earth

South Pole   southernmost end of the Earth

Read more

Arctic Ocean (Discover the Oceans), Emily Rose Oachs (Blastoff! Readers, 2017)

It's All About...Freezing Poles, Kingfisher (Kingfisher, 2015)

Polar Lands (Discover Science), Margaret Hynes (Kingfisher, 2017)

Websites

www.bbc.co.uk/nature/humanplanetexplorer/environments/arctic

http://discoveringantarctica.org.uk/

www.ducksters.com/geography/antarctic.php

Index

Antarctica 12

Arctic 6

days 18

Earth 4

feathers 14

foxes 10

fur 8

land 12

nights 20

North Pole 6

ocean 6

penguins 14

polar bears 8

poles 4, 18, 20

seals 16

snow 10

South Pole 12

summer 20

winter 18